UNDERSTANDING DIGITAL MARKETING

The principles of digital marketing explained simply and practically

Gilles Kroger

© Copyright: 2021 Gilles Kroeger

The work, including its parts, is protected by copyright. Any use without the consent of the publisher and the author is prohibited. This applies in particular to electronic or other copying, translation, distribution and making available to the public.

ISBN 978-1-304-68616-9

Gilles Kroeger
Ginsterweg 37
CH-4303 Kaiseraugst
Switzerland
Mail: kroeger.gilles@bluewin.ch

Foreword

Digital marketing is on everyone's lips these days. It seems that the whole world is turning faster and faster and more and more digital. Gone are the days when people were forced to watch advertising on television because they had no alternative. With the digital age, entirely new media and channels have been created.

New possibilities for companies to present themselves on different platforms and to show themselves in the best light. But digitalization also raises questions. The Internet is moving far too fast and for many, the digital transformation is both a blessing and a curse. The greatest challenge of our time will be to unite all age groups, ethnic groups, religions and world views and to shape the technologies of the future together.

The digital transformation has definitely begun. With this book I have tried to give an overview according to the current state of knowledge. It should be written for beginners, interested, advanced and all who deal with digital marketing.

Table of contents

BUSINESS MODEL INNOVATION 7

FACEBOOK 20

INSTAGRAM 23

YOUTUBE 26

LINKEDIN 29

Twitter / Pinterest / Tik Tok 32

PINTEREST 34

TIK TOK 35

VIDEO-MARKETING 36

VIDEO-MARKETING 58

STORYTELLING 60

CROSSMEDIA MARKETING 63

PERFORMANCE MARKETING 74

BANNERDESIGNS 82

NEUROMARKETING AND 85

CONVERSION RATE 85

OPTIMIZATION 85

SEARCH ENGINE MANAGEMENT 89

TARGETING 92

CRAWLING 94

INDEXING 94

PAGE LOADING TIMES 95

SEA (SEARCH ENGINE ADVERTISING) 96

DIGITAL ANALYTICS 100

Help through tools 102

WHAT ARE KPI (KEY PERFORMANCE INDICATORS) 105

LAW IN MARKETING AND COMMUNICATION 106

EPILOGU 115

BIBLIOGRAPHY 116

BUSINESS MODEL INNOVATION

Business Model Innovation impressively shows us the business model of the future and what we have to pay attention to in order to be successful. This can be services as well as goods in general. There are four elements for a successful business, which I would like to explain in more detail here:

Value Proposition: This is a value or value proposition. It describes what benefits a company promises its customers with a particular product or service.

Business structure: Setting up the structure required to generate added value and an experience for the customer. For example, supply, sales and communication, production, our core capabilities within the company, and the partners needed.

Revenue model: Here we ask ourselves what we ultimately earn money with. The cost structure is shown, as well as the actual revenue sources.

Entrepreneurship: Here we record what we can solve "in-house", for example, and for whom we as a company necessarily need an external partner. In general, the question arises here as to which competencies we possess in order to be able to meet the requirements.

Changes in the demands on business models

A good example to explain the changes in demands in a simple way is the Apple business empire. By the mid-1990s, Apple had fulfilled its niche of hardware and software to the point where profit growth was no longer readily achievable. From the year 2001 Apple started to bring a number of new and innovative products to the market.

This started with the IPod, followed by the ITunes music service, until finally the first IPhone saw the light of day. It was at this point, for example in our case of Apple, that the turning point began. It was recognized that the down-load market was lucrative, but it had long been neglected to develop innovative business models here. This realization made Apple suddenly a high flyer and within a few years the market leader in this area. (The Boston Consulting Group, Business Model Innovation)

The three horizons of innovation

In addition to the actual business models of Business Model Innovation, it is also important to look at the three horizons of innovation. Each of these individual stages requires different skills and also, depending on the stage, a different management understanding of the company. The characteristics of the individual horizons are also very different.

Basic concepts of the 3 horizons in business innovation

Horizon 1: This horizon concerns all current products and processes. Everything remains more or less the same as it was before. Our customers like and accept the current state of affairs. We are familiar with our competitors in the industry.

Horizon 2: Our current value chain and business model remains the same. Our customers are proactively exposed to new solutions, while existing expertise remains in place. At this level, business builders in leadership are required, as well as good sales people and innovatives.

Horizon 3: This horizon is the visionary part, if you will. It is very complex and difficult to implement. Competitors at this level are often startups, unknown, or non-industry business fields.

The 3-horizon model draws attention to a particular strategic challenge. While day-to-day business is handled on the horizon 1 level, companies must be active in parallel on horizon levels 2 and 3 in order to be able to successfully shape the future. (Dr. Hoffmann/J. / Rook/S., 18.03.2018)

The topic of business innovation demonstrated by a fictitious business case

Using the customer service project of XY AG, I will explain how the strategy can also be applied operationally and implemented in the corresponding subject areas.

Background information company XY

XY is one of the leading IT providers when it comes to digital transformation. Among other things, the company offers system integration, reverse services such as outsourcing processes, customer support tasks, and traditional consulting. The current problems at XY include the following:

Lack of innovation in the service area. Requests or problems were communicated via email instead of a ticketing tool.

Although the company calls itself a professional for digital transformation, it cannot pro-actively deliver new ideas to the customers, but the existing concept was quasi administered.

The business structure is entrenched in its cumbersome mechanisms and stalled processes. This prevented new ideas and innovations.

XY remains rigidly in the comfort zone (horizon 1) and does not even try to improve things or implement new ideas.

There is no external resource that can help to move forward in the digital area and to develop new innovations.

Due to these problems, it quickly becomes clear where the construction sites are to be found and what this would mean for the current and future business. An international project group was set up to identify additional problems within the Group so that everyone could start from the same starting point. The concept included points such as (budget, feasibility study, responsibilities and project goals). Furthermore, a requirements catalog was created to show which points had to be included and which could be added at a later point, or even deleted. Throughout the project, the focus was placed on the two points of the business innovation model and the 3 horizons of business innovation, and an attempt was made to implement these.

Project description and implementation of the individual steps

First, a company-wide and also customer-wide survey was launched to get a feeling of what customers want on the one hand and where the company stands internally. The result was exciting in that many customers and also internal employees came forward with the feeling of working in an old-fashioned company. This was due to the lack of innovation, as XY had mainly focused on managing the lived element instead of developing further.

After evaluating the survey and presenting it to the management, it was quickly realized that a large budget would be allocated to the area of customer service and innovation.
In order to be able to meet the technical challenges of the future, XY opted for modern ITSM software. This is quite expensive in terms of licenses, but it had the advantage that the interfaces could be adapted as deemed appropriate, independent of ready-made solutions, which many providers offer at a lower price. Another

Another advantage of this software that should not be underestimated was its ease of use and the possibility of creating added value for internal employees as well as for external customers.

With this simple step, XY has moved from the classic horizon 1 directly to horizon 2. In terms of employees, two new positions were created based on the experience gained with the interfaces in this short period of time to deal solely with this topic. One part was certainly the "usability" part, which should enable the user a comfortable "handling", but another one was the possibility to develop technically always further, independent from others. This has already changed a lot at XY today.

XY is currently much more sustainable in customer service (Wehrl/A. wie Business Model Innovation zu nachhaltigen Kundenbeziehungen führt), so that generally all requests on the platform can be processed by the new ITSM tool. In the past, customers XY sent mails for their problems or inquiries, which were then processed individually by someone.

Today, thanks to the powerful design of the platform, the employee or external customer can either send an e-mail as usual, but this is then converted directly into a ticket, making it measurable and evaluable. This process also provides the opportunity to build up a long-term knowledge base in the system, with which certain cases can be processed and intercepted in advance.

Customers can open trouble-relevant tickets on their own initiative, which can then be processed much more quickly due to a ka-tegorization of the ticket relevance. In the course of expanding the new ticket platform, the idea of integrating a kind of order store for hardware and software was born.

XY was otherwise asked by phone or e-mail to buy server X for company Y, or for example to get software Z and then make it available for a customer on all his devices. Here again, an internal project group met and decided to take the step from horizon 1 to horizon 2

Of course, we did not know whether all expectations could be met and whether the users would appreciate this. A start was made to include all servers, laptops, monitors, printers and other peripherals in the new ITSM tool in the form of an order option, similar to what is known in the e-commerce sector from a web store.

The customer or internal user now sees the orderable item visually in the form of a small icon and can order the desired item accordingly by double-clicking. At the end of the process there is a check-out system where all articles are listed again as a summary.

On the one hand, it shows the orderer once again clearly whether everything desired has been ordered, and on the other hand, the supervisor gets a kind of release option where he or she can then decide whether the order is justified and whether, in addition to budget planning, the order can be triggered in this way. If this is the case, a simple double-click is enough and the order is sent. The corresponding employee now receives a confirmation.

A start was made on recording all servers, laptops, monitors, printers and other peripheral devices in the new ITSM tool in the form of an order option, similar to what is known from the e-commerce area of a web store.

The customer or internal user now sees the available item visually in the form of a small icon and can double-click to order the desired item. At the end of the process there is a check-out system where all articles are listed again as a summary.

On the one hand, it shows the orderer once again clearly whether everything desired has been ordered, and on the other hand, the supervisor gets a kind of release option where he or she can then decide whether the order is justified and whether, in addition to budget planning, the order can be triggered in this way. If this is the case, a simple double-click is enough and the order is sent.

The corresponding employee receives a confirmation. The last point we will tackle in connection with the Business Innovation Model is a very topical one. XY serves customers in the insurance, banking and industrial sectors. Especially there, an above-average amount of paper is still being printed out, be it contracts or the like. In our "Horizon 1" process, the customers contacted XY when something was defective on the corresponding printer or had to be replaced. XY manage are supplied by company Z and made available.

We are now at the stage where Company Z's software is being linked to our ITSM platform. The advantage now clearly lies in setting the parameters for the printers. If this proves to be feasible, it would of course be a huge added value for all users. We could define key data via the system, for example when a printer cartridge is about to run out. Without the customer having to worry about it, either an order is triggered directly, or the customer is actively informed that the ink is about to run out. This gives customer service new opportunities to help shape the service level and take it to a higher level.

(Digital transformation requires business model inno-vation)

Summary of the "social media landscape

Need of the different platforms in the social media landscape

Each social media platform has its own goals and specific audience. Not only in terms of content, but also in the orientation of the corresponding service of the app, this can be represented as follows:

Publishing (for example) "Wikipedia"
Sharing (for example) "Spotify"
Messaging (for example) "Skype"
Discussing (for example) "Reddit"
Collaborating (for example) "Evernote
Networking (for example) "Tinder"

As we can see above, many social media platforms are specialized in their field. However, many large platforms, such as Face-book, LinkedIn, etc., have the advantage of enabling multiple orientations at the same time and thus reaching a much larger audience.

The most important social media platforms

If we look around our marketing environment, there are still some relevant platforms that stand out from the crowd. These would be Face-book, Instagram, YouTube, Twitter, LinkedIn, Pinterest and Tik Tok, among others. We will now look at these platforms in detail next and highlight the many advantages, but also the disadvantages, that each of these platforms brings with them. It should be mentioned that there are of course other big services like WhatsApp or Snapchat. But these will not be discussed further here in this framework, as it would go beyond it.

Weiss, J (2017), Die wichtigsten Socialmedia Plattfor-men- ein Überblick, retrieved from https://blog.mediakraft.de/some-uebersicht-86bec97a7d0c

FACEBOOK

The pros and cons of Facebook

Why is Facebook so successful and what exactly makes it so? One of the things that Facebook masters perfectly is certainly the diversity of its platform. You can quickly upload photos and comment on them, create groups for a wide variety of topics, and also communicate actively with the help of the already integrated messenger. With approximately 3.54 million people registered in Switzerland alone in the 1st quarter of 2020 according to Statista, the reach is very large and active.

Retrieved https://de.statista.com/statistik/daten/studie/70221/umfrage/anzahl-der-nutzer-von-facebook-in-der-schweiz/

The time spent on Facebook itself is also long, and around 66% of all monthly active users return to Facebook every day. If we move away from the private user and look at Facebook from a business perspective, we see that it is a very good advertising medium. What goals can you pursue with Facebook in marketing? It is of course the case that you can increase the level of awareness of your company. In addition to companies, this can also include products, brands, or even people. Another big plus of Facebook is customer loyalty. Here, various possibilities have been created to bring the customer closer to the company and to actively communicate with them.

Facebook also offers opportunities in the area of port, service and customer service and in customer loyalty to a specific product. For example, it is possible to actively ask the potential customer for his opinion about a product in order to understand what the customer would expect from the product and whether something can be optimized. A disadvantage of Facebook is that it collects a large amount of usable data about individual users, and it can never be completely guaranteed what will happen to them in the end. And this uncertainty can prevent one or the other Facebook user from logging in more often, or from making a wide variety of data public.

The 4 guiding principles in Facebook marketing

The 4 guiding principles of Facebook marketing can be summarized as follows

Create a social strategy
Leveraging an authentic brand voice
Create shareable content
Cultivate connections

With the above-mentioned guiding principles, a targeted marketing strategy can now be set up on Facebook. Depending on the company or enterprise, the goals are of a different nature. On the one hand, it may be that a specific product is to be promoted or awareness is to be generated for it. Also an increase of the traffic or the number of visitors can be a goal to apply the 4 guiding principles. An important point we have learned about Facebook should be:

Objectives can be extremely diverse. The goal should never be "Facebook only"!

INSTAGRAM

The pros and cons of Instagram

Instagram, like its big brother Facebook, is one of the most popular social media platforms. It is interesting to note that the percentage of men and women using Instagram in Switzerland is pretty much 50%. In contrast to Facebook, Instagram is oriented differently in that its main focus is on visual storytelling experiences. The main page of Instagram already shows what this means. Here, the user is not primarily attracted by the content, but much more by the images and videos.

Another reason why Instagram probably strikes a chord with users is that it works almost exclusively on mobile devices. Although there is now a desk-top version of Instagram, some of its functions are limited and not fully available. Instagram is also very strong in image and video editing using filters. The ability to customize your pictures and videos and change them according to your personal taste is one of the main reasons most users use Instagram.

You can play with emotions very well and this is certainly a decisive argument for the rapid growth that Instagram has experienced in recent years. One of the big disadvantages I personally see is the "fake followers" that have appeared in recent years.

There is, for money of course, the possibility to virtually push up his Instagram account with fake fans. In addition to the moral and ethical question, there is of course the general question of whether Instagram users will sooner or later leave the platform again, if there is an increasing feeling that something is not going on properly.

Instagram - platform orientation for companies

Possible applications for companies:

Most large companies and institutions can no longer afford to avoid Instagram these days. The platform has become too powerful and too many potential customers visit it. For companies, the benefits are as follows:

- Raising awareness / increasing attention for the company
- Arouse interest / make new customers aware of you with pictures and videos
- Customer acquisition / increase production sales
- Become personal / build fans and community

Here, too, the question ultimately arises as to which of the individual steps is suitable for one's company or enterprise. In the case of clothing stores, it would probably be more appropriate to promote a community or following for a specific brand, the proximity of the brand and target group, so to speak.

Of course, there is also the possibility to focus on sales and increasing sales. In this case, the focus is less on the community as a whole, but rather on trying to put the product in the right light so that more people will buy it. So we have seen that in the area of advertising, especially on Instagram, one or the other is possible.

Companies in particular have several options available here and can influence a lot of things, from increasing traffic to market research. Here, too, it will be important to try out a few things in order to find the best and most suitable means for yourself.

YOUTUBE

The pro and cons of YouTube

YouTube was founded in 2005 and has been part of the Google Group since 2006. YouTube is the portal for videos par excellence. All kinds of videos are published and consumed, e.g. film and TV clips, music videos, self-made products or tutorials on special hobbies or topics. Some facts, which "Brandwatch.com" has collected, are to be particularly emphasized. For example, YouTube is the second largest search engine, right behind Google.

The fact that the platform is available in 91 countries around the world and can interpret over 80 languages shows that YouTube is not listed as the second most popular social media platform in the statistics without good reason. Smith, K. (March 3, 2020) 57 interesting numbers and statistics about YouTube. Retrieved from https://www.brandwatch.com/de/blog/statistiken-youtube/

It has emerged that by 2020, about 80% of all Internet traffic will be generated on videos. However, there are also a few drawbacks to YouTube that need to be taken into account here.

On the one hand, YouTube reaches a lot of people, but not all of them. People over 50% visit the platform much less than younger people. It is also the case that many people find it difficult, or simply do not accept, to actively click on a website directly from YouTube, for example via advertising. From the point of view of a traffic source, YouTube is limited.

YouTube benefits for companies and businesses

Possible applications for companies

- The application possibilities for actively using YouTube in one's own company are extremely high. These would be for example:
- Brand awareness
- News for example about products and reports
- Instructions and explanations – Entertainment
- Use of the channel analogous to a television station

There are many functions within YouTube that can be interesting for companies. For example, it is generally possible to post videos up to a length of 15 minutes on YouTube. However, if the specific account is verified by YouTube, the length of the video can be much longer.

The "live streaming" feature can also be interesting to reach your audience quasi in real time. You have instant feedback and can also interact with the target audience immediately. This is, for example, a good tool to promote customer loyalty. If one is the rightful owner of a video, there is the possibility to activate the comment fields.

Due to this possibility, one immediately has a sense of how the video is received by the corresponding target persons. The whole thing is immediately recognizable via the "I like" and the "I don't like" function.

The "Playlist" is the last function we will take a look at regarding YouTubes. Playlists are collections of videos and can be created or shared. This has the advantage that you don't have to search for your favorite videos, which you might want to watch several times.

LINKEDIN

The pro and cons of LinkedIn

For me, LinkedIn was always something of a stepmother until this hour. I had an account there for quite some time and kept my data up to date as best I could, but I never really warmed up to the platform. This has changed since I saw what advantages it can offer. LinkedIn's platform orientation includes, among other things:

- Focus on the growth of the network
- Both personal and corporate profiles are possible
- Connecting professionals and like-minded people
- Generating leads

One of the big advantages, I think, is the LinkedIn learning platform, within LinkedIn itself. More than 15000 courses are offered, as well as various certification programs for various topics. The courses are paid, but as a countermove you get a certificate after successful completion, which is also directly visible in the profile.

What can be a disadvantage is that LinkedIn's premium functions are relatively expensive. And if you use them only partially, it is questionable whether the price is worth it. Benjamin, (June 26, 2019) LinkedIn for founders: do I need the network for my success? Retrieved from
https://www.fuer-gruender.de/blog/linkedin-fuer-gruender-basics/

LinkedIn benefits for companies and businesses

Possible applications for companies

It can be worthwhile for companies and businesses to advertise on LinkedIn. Various advertising formats allow a wide variety of advertising measures to be taken. For example, "Text Ads" can be used to increase the reach, to significantly increase brand awareness, or simply to generate more traffic and thus have an added value. With all advertising strategies that one would like to drive out of LinkedIn, it is important to note that there are also strict advertising guidelines that must be adhered to. These would include:

Tobacco advertising is strictly prohibited, no political content may be disseminated, or even religious content is strictly prohibited.

In this way, the platform wants to avoid risk groupings. If you have complied with the advertising guidelines and would like to run a campaign, we received one or two tips along the way that I found very valuable. In any case, you should choose high-resolution photos and images that immediately appeal to the "customer.

Low quality images can be off-putting or even unprofessional. It is also very important for the texts to appear appealing. The content can be decisive here. Advertising should be on LinkedIn for a markant amount of time than on Facebook, for example. Finally, I would like to mention the so-called "targeting".

This involves advertising measures that are tailored to a group of people or users. Thus, the reach of the campaigns can be extended here as well. So with targeting, we can specify exactly who we want to reach and in which sector.

For example, we can say that we want to target a specific city geographically, or we can specialize demographically by specifying the age of the people we want to target. The possibilities here are huge.

Twitter / Pinterest / Tik Tok

The pros and cons of Twitter / Pinterest and Tik Tok

I put these three platforms together because to me they represent the "small" group of the big socio-al media platforms, even though I'm probably doing them an injustice.

TWITTER

Twitter has a very high publication frequency, which distinguishes the platform from others. Especially in the area of "news", Twitter is usually even faster than the official news channels. With a maximum of 280 available characters, a tweet, i.e. a publication of a special content, can happen in real time.

However, there is also a major disadvantage due to the 280 characters. When it comes to complex issues, it becomes very difficult to present them in a comprehensible way on Twitter. It is also the case that the range is not particularly large and therefore the large masses cannot necessarily be reached. Bloom, D. (May 15, 2020). The pros and cons of Twitter. Retrieved from https://www.blumerang.com/die-vor-und-nachteile-von-twitter

PINTEREST

Pinterest is an online platform for graphics and images. A big advantage of Pinterest is that you can plan into the future, so to speak. For example, with Facebook, the view is always directed into the past with events or happenings, or in the present. With Pinterest, however, you are already looking into the future in the form of ideas, life events or similar.

The images, or pins, as they are called on Pinterest, can also be used for marketing purposes in the form of advertising. Over half of Pinterest users, do not know that it is an ad. Customers generally have a high purchase intention when they search for inspiration and ideas on Pinterest. As a disadvantage, it can be pointed out that the spread of Pinterest is not yet very high and the advertising functions are not yet really mature.

TIK TOK

Surprisingly, Tik Tok does not come from the USA, but from China. The platform is intended for watching and distributing short video clips. Tik Tok has a huge reach and is present in over 150 countries with over 75 different languages available. The time spent on the site is around 40 minutes per day per user.

Why should Tik Tok be used today from a business and marketing perspective? On the one hand, the next generation has found joy in this platform and uses it regularly and often. The creativity of the users and the awareness is very high on this platform and this can be directly converted into marketing-relevant content in this way.

However, Tik Tok also has disadvantages that cannot be glossed over. Since China is the manufacturer of the platform, you never know exactly what happens with your own data. Since the marketing and advertising portion is still very limited, companies should consider whether it makes sense to advertise on Tik Tok.

The platform itself is not yet very well known in the German-speaking countries (Germany, Austria and Switzerland). This can be a disadvantage if you lose interested customers to other platforms or are generally not perceived as an independent brand on Tik Tok.

VIDEO-MARKETING

Corporate Video-Marketing

In today's world, where smartphones are ubiquitous, it is no longer enough to simply be present on the "net". Some time ago, images were more important than videos on the platforms, but this has now changed dramatically.

If you want to motivate customers to be interested in products and purchases, videos are already ahead. (Theobald, 2018) While at the beginning of the social media era a few blurred images in poor quality were enough to impress customers, today time has not stood still here either.

To produce high-quality films and videos, it is advisable to invest in a good camera, among other things. It guarantees a high resolution incl. full format sensor, which is best suited for the creation of videos. Another point that is often underestimated is the tripod. Only the tripod can ensure that the footage is not shaky and smooth. An important point with videos is always the sound.

The best film is expressionless if all you hear is static on the line. For this reason, it is recommended to invest in good speech microphones. Best suited are for example XLR microphones, which are used together with the appropriate XLR cables. There is also a lot to consider when it comes to lighting, so that the results are coherent in the end. Mobile lamps can help to illuminate rooms. Also a so-called white balance should be made in advance, because otherwise the recorded people look pale, or even unnaturally brown colored.

A good service is provided by LED lamps that are mounted directly on the corresponding tripod. The influence on the image quality can change very positively. It is also possible to purchase a so-called green screen.

This is a special piece of green cloth, which is built in the background. With this technology, background photos or various graphics can be inserted later. The advantage of the green screen technology is that photos can be realized cheaply. Also, the flexibility remains high, especially if you want to project different background images, or also work in the creative field with special effects.

In any case, it is important to realize that you will get much higher quality footage if you take the abovementioned things into account and try to achieve as perfect a video result as possible.

The topic of social media demonstrated by a fictitious business case of company XY

Practical application of Facebook

As an IT outsourcer and consulting firm, XY has many external customers who are also IT-savvy, so they thought about how they could integrate Facebook into everyday life. Customers often have XY on the phone, especially in the service desk/customer service, but no picture and no impression in the form of people. It was hoped that Facebook would create an even closer emotional bond between the customers and the company by radiating a certain closeness.

XY set up a company homepage in Facebook so that every employee could register himself. The added value was there after just a few days. The customers now have an emotional closeness to the support and feel "much more relaxed." A topic called "behind the scenes" is also communicated via Facebook. For example, upcoming maintenance windows for systems are discussed, where users and customers can have their say. On the one hand, XY has received the feedback that they as a company accompany the customer with his ideas and also concerns and that the customer is not virtually presented with the finished product. The power of co-decision has a positive effect on the number of telephone calls, as measured by various internal statistics.

The accessibility of the clientele has also changed to some extent. There are of course still the "classics" who still pick up the phone, but feedback has also been sent via Messenger, accounting for about 40% of the total daily volume.

XY currently has an official homepage of the company, including the range of services, as well as the Face-book page, which is now rapidly gaining popularity, as XY itself notes. I found an interesting online blog article about this, which pretty much describes what we find as advantages and disadvantages of Face-book in comparison to regular homepages. Mitter, S. (2020).

Website vs. Facebook - The advantages- & disadvantages for SMEs. Retrieved from https://www.prospega.de/de/mediaratgeber/fachartikel/facebook-vs-webseiten-kmu

Advertising also plays a major role for us as Company XY. In addition to software and digital transformation services, they also provide hardware. The idea is now to place corresponding advertisements for the available hardware within the Facebook page in order to show the customer what other options are available in addition to the services he has already ordered. Due to the interactive chat in Messenger or directly in the Facebook platform itself, new options for an additional sale of devices or the like arise.

What we have noticed in relation to company XY because of Facebook is that XY is perceived as moder because there is an increased focus on Facebook. This may be related to the fact that customers and users of this platform also associate something positive with it in their private lives and therefore deal with it very impartially. In general, it seems that customers with IT problems or incidents are also more patient when communicating via Facebook.

A survey of fictitious users was conducted in this regard and the conclusion was that the Facebook platform, as it is used at company level, gives users the feeling of being advised and supported more quickly and competently. In terms of the user's patience for complex problems, it has also been shown that Facebook communicates well due to the feeling of closeness to the people and that the customer waits longer for the solution without becoming impatient.

Practical application of Instagram

The importance of Instagram can no longer be underestimated, even by companies today. So we thought about what we as company XY could do in terms of Instagram and what our customers would be interested in. Since we are a big team and many of our customers don't know what kind of people work at XY and who is responsible for what, XY decided to do a round of introductions. Each of the XY employees, who wanted to and agreed, presented a short video about the function they have in the company.

At the end of the action there were about 300 videos from different departments. It started with SAP and ended with the service desk and customer service. We discreetly added the logo of company XY to the individual videos so that there was a direct link to it.

The goal was quite simply "brand awareness" in this case. In Instagram, we opened an account on the company name and made sure that the company could deliver good and interesting content. But it is also important for us to show the customer what XY does, how professionally it is done and how diverse the company is.

It also puts the focus on the employees' know-how and gives viewers a completely new picture and new ideas about XY. In the meantime, customers really appreciate that XY is represented on Instagram. The company frequently receives feedback and comments about the individual videos that are created. In return, XY also encourages users to send their biggest challenges and problems with computer software and hardware so that they can be worked out in the form of videos for all users.

We opened the account on our company name XY in Instagram and since then we have been looking to deliver good and interesting content. However, it is also important for us to show the customer what we do, how professionally we do it and how diverse we are. This also puts the focus on the know-how of the employees and gives the viewers a completely new picture and new ideas about XY Company.

Meanwhile, customers really appreciate that the company is on Instagram. Often, XY gets feedback and comments about the individual videos that have been created. The big goal from a customer service perspective was to generate fewer phone calls by transferring knowledge via Instagram in the form of short videos. This goal has already been met, with an estimated 10% decrease in calls.

In return, a strong community has formed within Instagram, who also exchange knowledge topics with each other or proactively help other users by writing solutions in the comments. This goes in the direction of customer work, where the customer acts as a teacher or salesperson. It could also be determined that new customers were added because they first noticed company XY on Instagram and then contacted them in the traditional way.

Company XY has been actively focusing on Instagram Stories for about two weeks now and has been posting them regularly. This has proven to be efficient in the area of maintenance work on computer systems or update intervals, which also have to be carried out regularly by XY. Firsching, J. (November 14, 2018). Instagram Stories. How companies should use Instagram Stories.

Retrieved from
https://www.futurebiz.de/artikel/instagram-stories-tipps-unternehmen/

in the area of maintenance work on computer systems, or update intervals, which must also be performed regularly by XY. Firsching, J. (November 14, 2018). Instagram Stories. How businesses should use Instagram Stories.
Retrieved from
https://www.futurebiz.de/artikel/instagram-stories-tipps-unternehmen/

One is now able to quickly, modernly and entertainingly inform about processes that affect and influence the entire community of XY. Another question we are currently looking at from a commercial perspective is the possibility of advertising within Instagram. The idea would be, for example, to run a "Carousel Ads" to not only reach our already existing audience, but also to open up other business areas beyond that. XY offers hardware especially for banks and insurance companies, as well as the corresponding peripherals.

The Carousel Ads would be perfect for this. XY could arouse interest in the product, as well as drive and expand customer acquisition. This inevitably leads to more traffic on the Instagram account, as well as a planned increase in sales of the individual products. IGTV, the video platform of Instagram, is also another topic that our company XY has started to deal with.

With a maximum video running time of 60 minutes, it is of course very tempting to offer something there in the form of tutorials or training. One is not so rushed in terms of time and can count on a large existing audience. Company XY will soon publish its first tutorial on the topic of "Integrating Instagram into the existing service desk structure of insurance companies".

Practical application of YouTube

Since YouTube was introduced in 2005, it quickly became clear to XY that it would be a great opportunity to do something in the area of advertising and customers. It is probably in the nature of things that the moving images turned out to be much more attractive than the conventional standard photos. Another advantage for us is that the videos can be translated into different languages and thus the same content can be conveyed internationally.

As a main focus, XY decided to provide customers with tutorials and explanatory videos on the most frequently asked problems or questions. For this reason, a channel was started on YouTube with a collection of different topics.

XY has started a survey among customers and partners to find out which are the IT topics that are repeated or which cause the most problems in the daily work. The idea is followed up by the fact that XY will be able to make individual videos for its premium or VIP customers, to answer their questions and to provide tips and explanations. Last week XY had a live streaming for the first time with a group of ten people about the problem of connecting printers to the local network of the companies.

In addition to training documents and explanations by the relevant technician, the company was also able to respond directly to the questions that arose. Thus, the learning effect was almost 100% and the customers were more than satisfied. They found the variant innovative and up-to-date. What was not our intention, but is a nice side-effect of the videos and live-streamings, is the range expansion of the audience, as well as a positive effect on brand awareness.

XY has circulated some videos, which were suddenly shared and XY suddenly completely unknown companies have written to, whether they could also help them, as we have shown in the videos as an example. So here, too, we basically fulfilled the advertising goals that need to be implemented on YouTube. There were definitely several leads generated that also want to work with XY in the long term.

The traffic on the individual videos was also increased above-average from our expectations as a result. The question now arises as an international company, what XY could do in the area of "branding" on YouTube. After some research, we found good information for the individual topics and how they can be implemented. Chen. (October 3, 2017). Tips on branding your YouTube chan-nel. Retrieved from https://artplusmarketing.com/tips-on-branding-your-youtube-channel-3f67f4f2ca00

Along with embedding the company logo, XY has come to the conclusion that classic advertisements are also a mundane means of monetizing the effort or, in any case, making the company better known. Because the problem with XY is still that although XY is a group, it is practically not perceived as an IT service provider or even as an outsourcer. We started to implement the advertising ourselves with the classic display ad at the top right of the video.

However, XY quickly realized that this was counterproductive, as most users use tabs or their cell phones to access YouTube videos. Display viewing, on the other hand, only works on desktop computers. XY also briefly tested YouTube's over-lay display feature. However, customers found these to be quite intrusive and pushing.

And these are also only supported on desktop computers, which gave two minus points for the form. In the end, Company XY as a whole came to the conclusion that they would agree on the "Skippable Video Display" and the "Non-Skippable Video Display". The advantages were obvious because both variants of the ad formats could also be integrated on mobile devices and tablets, ensuring that the ads would reach the appropriate audience.

At the moment, XY is still in the test phase, but it is already clear that we can reach people with the advertising. Especially the advertising sequence before the regular tutorials has already brought XY some additional product purchases and leads.

Practical application of LinkedIn

I'll be blunt and admit that until recently, our company XY didn't really think much about LinkedIn. Of course, the platform had been around for a long time and one or two of the employees had an account on it, but in detail, for XY, it was simply a "job search" platform, as there are several. In the process, it escaped our notice that we could have good advertising opportunities on LinkedIn as a company, while also expanding our network in general. The first thing XY did was to create its own company page on LinkedIn. The first thing they did was to look at the "Hire Talent Solutions" section. There, more and more recruiters have become aware of us and are now looking for personnel in the market specifically according to our job requirements.

This platform costs our company XY some money and budget per month, but with more than 15000 courses currently offered, the price-performance ratio is very good. Another point we wanted to improve was and is our "Brand Awareness" of the company. This was generally too little represented online and with the company page we have proactively done something here. By means of text ads and video ads on the site, the reach could be increased significantly.
Franklin, J. (September 4, 2019). How to effectively use LinkedIn for brand awareness.
Retrieved from https://themanifest.com/social-media/how-effectively-use-linkedin-brand-awareness

In any case, it is clear that the platform continues to grow, and XY notices this in its daily use of the platform.

Another point that we as company XY now often use is the learning platform "LinkedIn learning" This is an interactive training option. From individual courses that can be viewed on video to complete daylong training courses, everything is available. The certification programs are particularly popular with our employees, where knowledge is also conveyed with the help of question options, similar to a classroom.

We also notice time and again that LinkedIn is constantly developing these further and becoming more innovative. In the next six months, we will increase the advertising activity on LinkedIn as company XY and keep the advertising switched on longer than on Facebook, for example. Lead generation in general will also be pushed and expanded. We have now firmly integrated this platform, which we underestimated, into our everyday marketing work at XY and see the potential that is hidden there, even in the B2B sector.

Practical application of Twitter

At XY, we use Twitter specifically for our service desk and customer service. We chose Twitter for service desk communication with our customers because it offers several advantages that other platforms don't have. For one thing, spreading new messages is straightforward. With 280 characters you have enough possibilities to share the most important news that our customers need as information (Tweet).

Our customers appreciate this very much, as it is perceived as innovative and modern, and we have been able to increase customer satisfaction by quite a bit as a result. It is also noticeable that we have already been able to stimulate some discussions with Twitter and that this has also led to exciting conversations and interactions between us as a company and our customers. What we have introduced since last week, for example via Twitter, is a weekly short tweet that we send out as a service desk to the customers of company XY.

It contains short and concise information about the upcoming maintenance windows of the systems and from when to when they will not be available. What we also appreciate is the quick feedback regarding newly introduced services. We recently carried out a company-wide update of SAP and wanted to find out from the employees concerned how it works?

The users felt that they were being listened to and heard. They can also give us feedback on the need for adjustments and changes in the individual departments.

We are glad that we have Twitter as a platform and can communicate so quickly and easily. It is a high-quality network that we would like to expand in the future.

Practical application of Pinterest

Pinterest has never really been a topic at Company XY. However, we have now also started to use this platform to find out whether it has an additional benefit for us. The biggest advantage of the platform is certainly its focus on the future. With other platforms like Instagram or Facebook, we either look to the past or to the present.

With Pinterest, however, we are looking to the future. Since the purchase intention in Pinterest is particularly high, it was important for us as a company to be present there and to actively participate. We have set up a Pinterest company page to take full advantage of the platform. We have created boards with new hardware components and generated various pins.

What is particularly interesting for us as a company, of course, with the appropriate SEO optimization, is the indexing together with Google. The organic reach can also be and has already been increased, which also speaks for Pinterest as a platform. Strong, N. (December 4, 2018). 6 benefits of Pinterest for your business. Retrieved from https://www.pergenz.de/blog/6-vorteile-von-pinterest-fuerunternehmen/

Practical application of Tik Tok

We have included Tik Tok as the latest social media platform in our offering. It was important for the company to also be able to address the younger generation, as these are the customers of tomorrow, so to speak. Unfortunately, I have to say that we at XY as an IT company quickly reached the limits of Tik Tok. After all, it is a platform that, by chance, does not come from the USA for once, but was launched directly in China.

Since we are obligated to ensure that no data migrates or is intercepted in places that we do not consider trustworthy, we have a practical problem for this reason alone. In addition, we have found that the level of awareness in our German-speaking countries is not yet very pronounced. Especially our fictitious companies in the DACH association quickly reach their limits here. Advertising itself is still in its infancy and will have to develop further.
However, we have to admit that the actual usage time of the users on this platform is very high. We have now started, as a company, to create small videos in the form of employees, which should show in a funny, creative and innovative way, what is the field in which they work and how they are doing. The next project on Tik Tok will be to show the offices of XY, again in a fun way. Our goal will be to attract new young customers, who will see an identification through the videos and will be interested in our company and our products.

Social media for company XY in summary

In this section, I would like to once again point out all the aspects that social media has in connection with company XY. In the past, the company failed to jump on the new platforms and actively participate in them. This brought with it various disadvantages, including XY being classified as old-fashioned and conservative. We have now improved this and clearly see the benefit and also the positive of being active on the various platforms.

We are now where our target group is, which was not always the case before. When we think about Twitter, we understand that we now have active dialogs and exchange with our customers. Customers feel closer to the product and to us as a business and a company. With Facebook, we've now been able to generate advertising revenue that wasn't even on our radar before.

This alone has made it worthwhile to invest. Through our company page on LinkedIn, we have been able to hire about five new employees in the last three weeks, simply because LinkedIn was able to link our requirements to the existing open positions. What is positive is that the reach of customers has become much larger than before the social media adjustments. We have without a doubt also managed to give a face to our brand and our brand as XY.

The company is now more noticed and almost gets human traits. We created the campaign on Tik Tok with the employees, who all shared something about their work in a very short time. This was very well received, as it virtually humanized our label, with all its facets. So we generated also, many new followers and fans, who understand themselves in the meantime already as loyal customers of our services. It is also not easy to maintain and develop the presence of a company. We have implemented this with social media elements and will continue to do so.

We recently started offering a weekly newsletter in the form of a post on Facebook. This contains information about what is currently going on internally, what is planned for the next few weeks and what projects are currently being worked on. Our customers have already confirmed that this post conveys a sense of togetherness and that they feel part of the big picture. Lawal, M. (August 1, 2018). 23 benefits social media offers businesses. Retrieved from https://blog.hootsuite.com/de/vorteile-von-social-media-fuer-unternehmen/

Let's talk about the topic of influencers and Instagram. Last week, we started a fictitious cooperation with an influencer from the video game industry. His goal is to find as many people as possible to join him in discussing and criticizing the latest games. We have now been able to place an advertisement that promotes a desktop PC specifically for "gaming". The beauty of this is that the influencer is now playing with our PC and our "brand" is extremely visible on the PC.

This alone has boosted the sales of this model very much and has the nice side effect that people generally inform themselves about us. Be it on other social media platforms or directly on the net. So, from a marketing point of view, we have managed to boost PC sales with little effort, just through Instagram. Because of this success, management has taken notice and wants to gradually increase the budget for social media activities. On my advice, a concept is also being developed for what to do and communicate in the event of a crisis situation. What I learned a lot from the lessons and what definitely stuck with me was: It has to be communicated quickly and correctly. It is no use for a company to keep quiet about problem cases, because in the end they are still not solved for everyone.

So what needs to be communicated clearly is what has happened? What restrictions does it have for the customers? What happens in the meantime and when is it resolved? To me, this sounded so trivial, but we also realized the consequences of not communicating honestly and laly. In the meantime, our customer service has hired a social media manager who takes care of the whole platform process, but also of the current content feeds and news.

For example, he handles the tweets on Twitter, which we now post regularly and have hit the bull's eye with based on a survey of opinions. In addition, our customer service team will work more with Facebook and will increasingly draw attention to our services and opportunities there as well. One last point that I would like to mention here is the direct feedback from customers regarding hardware and services, which we receive via the social media platforms and can then actively evaluate at our company. This is how we establish the best satisfaction.

VIDEO-MARKETING

Corporate Video Marketing

In this day and age when smartphones are ubiquitous, it is no longer enough to simply be present on the "net". Some time ago, images on the platforms were more important than videos, but this has now changed dramatically. If you want to motivate customers to buy a product and interest in buying, videos are already ahead. (Theobald, 2018) While at the beginning of the social media era a few blurred images in poor quality were enough to impress customers, today time has not stood still here either.

To produce high-quality films and videos, it is advisable to invest in a good camera, among other things. It guarantees a high resolution incl. full format sensor, which is best suited for the creation of videos. Another point that is often underestimated is the tripod. Only the tripod can ensure that the footage is not shaky and smooth. An important point with videos, is always the sound. The best film is expressionless, if you only hear a hissing in the universe. For this reason, it is recommended to invest in good speech microphones. Best suited are, for example, XLR microphones, which are used together with the appropriate XLR cables.

There is also a lot to consider when it comes to lighting so that the results are coherent in the end. Mobile lamps can help to illuminate rooms. A so-called white balance should also be made in advance, because otherwise the recorded people will look pale, or even unnaturally brown.

A good service is provided by LED lamps mounted directly on the corresponding tripod. The influence on the image quality can change very positively. It is also possible to purchase a so-called green screen. This is a special piece of green cloth, which is set up in the background. With this technology, background photos or various graphics can be inserted later.

The advantage of green screen technology is that it is cheap to produce images. Also, the flexibility remains high, especially if you want to project different background images or work with special effects in the creative field. In any case, it is important to realize that you will get much higher quality footage if you take the above-mentioned things into account and try to achieve the most perfect video result possible with it.

STORYTELLING

Storytelling for business

To put a service or product in the proverbial spotlight with potential customers, it takes more than a chaotic video without a plan or plot. This is where so-called storytelling comes into play. It is actually a kind of script or roadmap where you try to sell a story including emotions similar to a feature film. The story, i.e. the story, should contain certain components such as originality, relevance, excitement, identification and topicality, to name but a few.

(Teamblau, 2020) There are also some factors which make a story interesting for the consumer. One is to create a possibility of identification with the main figure. The suspense should succeed in such a way that the consumer and customer join in the excitement and continue to be "hooked" on the video.

If the suspense is present from the beginning to the end, the willingness to watch the video will also be much greater. Everyday events are also always a plus point in storytelling. When consumers realize that there are no superheroes in the video, but people like "you and me", together with the events that can happen to anyone, the connection to the story is much closer.

In this context, the story should also be told truthfully. Even if there were stumbling blocks in the venture, you can include them without hesitation. This makes the story authentic for everyone. Although videos are often time-consuming and can also cost a lot of money, it is worth taking this route.

When we talk about conversation rates, we see that it's almost 80 percent plus in the video segment, as opposed to traditional images. Also, "sharing", i.e. sharing on other platforms, usually goes up to ten times more. The form of "how-to" videos stands out in particular. Customer satisfaction increases markedly when it is understood how this type of video can be used. If the company includes a video on its own website, the conversation rate also increases by up to 80 percent than on the classic website. SEO, or Search Engine Optimization, is also a big issue with videos.

It should be noted that video-optimized websites are listed and thus displayed much higher on the common search engines than the classic ones. A good tip is to launch a message to its video community at the end of the film. The consumers should be encouraged to leave a message, rate the video or visit a special website.

These actions quickly provide information about the behavior of consumers and customers. So what kind of video is suitable for a company? Good stories are always when a look behind the scenes can be taken, or employees report with a personal story and their experiences with the company or the enterprise. Also a production process of a product can be exciting to capture in the video. Especially if the normal customer otherwise does not have the opportunity to see these processes.

Old-established and traditional companies often also make videos about their founding history and the historical aspects of the company. In that move, they can also mention company values that can be woven into the video.

Something important for me, which I have taken from the lessons, is that the videos are usually watched without sound, for example, because you do not want to disturb anyone with the smartphone, or simply do not have the time to linger on the video for a long time. For this reason, the video should be understandable even without sound, or if this is not possible, subtitles should be included so that the consumer does not refrain from watching the video.

CROSSMEDIA MARKETING

Crossmedia marketing in companies

What does cross-media marketing mean for companies? In the past, companies had a strategy. For example, campaigns were carried out in the analog media sector (mailings, posters, advertisements, brochures, etc.). The hope was to reach as large an audience as possible, but without knowing in detail how the campaign was measurably successful. Today, one would proceed differently, i.e. crossmedially.

To implement such a cross-media marketing strategy, one goes through the following processes to reach a large field of potential leads. Cross-media marketing opens up new opportunities to distribute content across multiple communication channels. Previously, consumption of content on one communication channel ended as soon as the recipient moved away from the sending channel. (Hilker, n.d.)

First, a target group is defined with which the cross-media campaign is to be run. Here, an intersection between storytelling and crossmedia can also be established. What is important here is the common thread of the story and that the story is coherent.

A very important point is to make the correct media choice. It makes no sense to prefer YouTube, for example, if the customers and consumers are all on Instagram and LinkedIn. You have to set clear goals right from the start as to which platform should be used and linked to which customers.

Another very important point, in my personal opinion, is the possibility of interaction in these campaigns. I want to have the opportunity to be actively involved in something and to be able to participate.

"How-to tutorials" video marketing in XY company

As I said, company XY hasn't really been out and about in terms of video marketing. We first thought about what kind of added value we could help the customers with by means of videos. In the past, when hardware was adapted, for example when a printer was replaced, documentation was provided in paper form.

This sometimes came across as "old-fashioned" to customers, or the text was written in such a technical way that customers were practically forced to call the service desk again anyway. From a marketing and commercial point of view, the longer the paper booklet was used, the less sense it made.

It cost a lot of money, as we had to print out about 2000 instructions in paper form, especially when replacing printers, to name one example. Apart from environmental issues, the time that one of the employees had to spend on this was of course not really very satisfying. So we made a cost calculation (paper, employee time, nerves and unhappy customers) and went to the fictitious management of XY with it.
We were able to quickly show that the way of documentation in paper form should be over. Especially in the area of server technology, the documentation became more and more confusing and useless. Fortunately, we have a management at XY that trusts us and lets us do most of the work.

The branding budget for an improvised film studio was approved very quickly. It was set up in our old internal computer center, which is no longer needed and is out of operation anyway. We decided to work with green screen, because there we also have the possibility to work with special background options or special effects. (Pilot, 2019)

We started from the point of view that we should buy something qualitatively better in terms of camera and equipment from the beginning, so that the final result is also satisfactory and can be shown to the customer without any problems.

The following considerations and purchases we have taken into account for the video production:
For the lighting, the spotlights already installed from the old days came to our aid. These were already directed towards the ceiling and produced an indirect light source. However, we still bought a classic studio lamp, because one side of the room always felt a little brighter than the other. This was probably due to the asymmetrically installed ceiling lamps. With the studio lamp, we were able to fade the contrast perfectly by placing the lamp slightly to the right and providing additional light. In a second test, the image appeared perfectly illuminated.

In terms of professional microphones, we found a good compromise between price and performance. It was very important to us that the microphones could individually mask out any background noise, for example running PC computers or server noise. This is possible with our new three microphones without any problems and can be implemented well.

When we were looking for a suitable camera tripod, we weren't sure at the beginning whether it should be a flexible one that can be swiveled manually or a classic tripod-style one. We had the opportunity to test both versions in our studio and finally stuck with the tripod. It is easy to assemble and can be used so individually that it was a sensible decision to buy one.

Another sticking point for us was deciding which camera and, above all, which type of camera to start with. After various tests, we came to the conclusion that the smartphone can offer very good quality, but that it is no match for a conventional high-quality camera, especially in the studio. The smartphone is mainly at a disadvantage when it comes to fast light changes and movements. So we bought a pro-fic camera for filming and have not regretted it so far. The quality speaks for itself and the entire video looks very high quality and professional.

After we had worked through all these points, we could almost get down to business. Only a small challenge we still had with enough power connections. It is unbelievable how many plugs you have when all the listed devices and helpers are in use. As luck would have it, an update of the existing printers of our main customer had to be done in the next few weeks. Normally this would mean that we would have to update about 500 printers and hope that the customers would be able to carry out the individual steps with the help of the documentation. Unfortunately, we cannot do this remotely. This means that in the event of problems or non-functioning updates, IT is done by sneaker, i.e. we go directly by.

This time it was to be that we, as a service desk, would shoot a video to determine whether this type of communication would also be well received by the customer. If the video was successful, we would start up the studio as a new source of information, so to speak. Since we had no experience with video in the past, we got help from an expert for our first attempt. He instructed us in handling, lighting and movement and showed us how to get the best result. As a "how-to update" main actor, one of our apprentices agreed to step in front of the camera. We wanted a young uncomplicated face in front of the camera and not a proven technician, so that the viewer also feels picked up. (https://digitalmarketinginstitute.com/, n.d.)

Now it was time to write a script for the corresponding video. We had to make sure that the relevant processes involved in this update were all explained in the video and paraphrased as simply as possible. We started by dividing the film into different segments. First, there was going to be an introduction explaining why we switched to video. Then the main character, our apprentice, should talk about himself, why he is making the video and what he wants to give to the viewers. Next came the actual content, the technical part, so to speak.

Here it was very important to us as company XY that the video is authentic and that it is delivered in such a way that the viewer does not look like the "stupid one" but is included. Since the technicians and programmers have been too much in the matter for years and usually don't understand the simple user, we decided to invite the boss of the customer to tell us what information his employees need to make the update as simple as possible.
Surprisingly, he came to our studio with keywords and talked bilaterally with the apprentice. The script had to end with the solution of the update and with a funny and interesting end-credit for the viewer. We wanted to achieve that the customer looks forward to another video and then enjoys watching it. The shoot itself then started with a practice run. We first had to get used to the whole scenario, but after a good hour, we slowly got into the swing of things. We added funny anecdotes to the video and after a good two hours we were ready to go.

Within hours including editing, the film was in the can. Now we had to inform the customers that the video would be available in YouTube format for this printer update. Since we had no idea, due to lack of experience, how the customers would react, we went into the race somewhat old-fashioned, by means of a newsletter. The newsletter included a link to watch the video and explain why we were switching to video.

The newsletter was sent out and we knew from old updates that of the approximately 500 users contacted, a little less than half would come back to our customer service with questions. The feedback was more than gratifying and amazing. We had a quota of about 40 users, but virtually all of them were happy to see the video first. Of course, we were very pleased about this great response and it confirmed our decision to further expand and initiate this type of communication.

Crossmedia marketing in company XY

We have now learned as a company that it is absolutely worthwhile to switch to video marketing. The question we asked ourselves was how far we could go cross-media. What would be the added value for the customers and also for us as company XY? The classic mail newsletter with the embedded video link worked well, but it was decided to go one step further and make the filmed movies available as a YouTube channel. XY knew that customers have an affinity for YouTube and that it would take less effort to click on the video there than on the internal mail. At the same time, the company's Facebook page was also revised, so that the latest videos were highlighted in the news.

On the company's internal website, we have set up a countdown when the next video from us will appear. This has also shown measurable success. Meanwhile, XY produces about three videos per week with a length of five to 15 minutes, depending on the topic. We have broadened and expanded our customer base to include our other clients. Although this is not our core competence, we generated a new service for a smaller SME customer of ours. This was done at the request of the customer and is currently very profitable for the company. The service is called "Video as a service" and makes us quasi film producers. The customer wants a video about topic XY for his employees.

So he comes to us and we, with our newly acquired expertise, give him the script he wants. At the same time he can shoot and edit his video in our studio. In addition to the regular income, we also have the advantage that we complement each other well from a digital marketing perspective in the area of social media. Our two companies send "likes" on Instagram, liken the videos on YouTube and write comments. However, with more experiential data we've now been able to gather, we've also noticed what doesn't work for our company, for example. The LinkedIn platform never really took off for us in terms of videos. (Marketingimpott.de, 2020)

This is also often due to the fact that customers in particular are no longer specifically fixated on our company XY when they look at LinkedIn. There it shifts to people and networking activity mainly. We have now moved away from LinkedIn in the area of video promotion and announcement again. A next big step will be to make our ticket system "ITSM" ready for videos. There is a corresponding plugin, which will be activated next month at XY. The goal will be to support the existing know-ledge base, i.e. solution paths of already closed tickets, with video. On the one hand, it will be very convenient for the end customer to use the search function to follow up on any questions that may arise by clicking on a video.

We are currently in a test phase with about 30 users in this area. The procedure is that when a fault occurs or a question arises about a computer system or similar, a ticket is sent to our service desk. In the past, the service desk agent looked at the ticket and then decided whether it should be sent to a programmer, to the SAP team, or whether it should remain with him for processing. What is new is that a database with the videos is stored on the servers. These are rotated or actualized when the topic requires it.

If the questioner now sends a mail to our mail address, this generates a ticket with a number in ServiceNow. ITSM itself now has a filter that searches for keywords and whole sentences. If the search is positive, the questioner is automatically sent a mail with some videos as a suggestion. If the corresponding video is included, which would solve the problem, the user can watch it directly from the mail by clicking on the link. Otherwise he clicks on a button and we contact him by phone. He also has the possibility to send us feedback, if he would like to have a video for a special topic. We take this on our hit list and then implement the Videos in our studio. The experience speaks for itself, at least so far. Customers find it very innovative and are practically already looking forward to the funny and well-made videos.

PERFORMANCE MARKETING

What defines Performance Marketing?

When we talk about performance marketing, what exactly is it about? Performance marketing is an online marketing tool that allows you to trigger measurable responses from customers or transactions accordingly.

Characteristics of Performance Marketing

In performance marketing, we have some important characteristics that show what needs to be observed accordingly. The measurability of the individual actions carried out can be evaluated and assessed in real time. Through adjustments, such as texts, images and also bids, various fine adjustments can be carried out and optimized. In this way, the success of the current campaign can be directly influenced. Performance marketing often interacts with classic marketing campaigns. The awareness of an individual brand, for example, has an impact on the success of the campaign in both performance marketing and traditional marketing. (https://www.cyberclick.net/marketing/performance-marketing/, n.d.)

Important terms of the pricing models of performance marketing

In the field of performance marketing, we know of various pricing models that can be used and which I would like to describe here:

CPM/TKP (cost per mille / price per thousand contacts) With this price model, the number of contacts is counted by the thousand, as it were, and also billed in this way. With the help of an ad server, the number of contacts is counted and billed accordingly. The prices for this type of pricing model are highly dependent on the corresponding placement of the advertising. In general, it can be said that prices between CHF 10 and CHF 120 are considered common in the industry.

Fixed placement In the case of fixed placement, one rents a space for a certain period of time, for example for X weeks or specific days. This placement is often not exclusive for someone, but is shared with a percentage factor, with other customers. This is certainly one of the weaknesses of this pricing model. The traffic generated in this way cannot be tracked one hundred percent. So you can only guess how promising this method is and a more precise analysis is almost impossible. Professional providers, however, give a guarantee on the corresponding insertions. This is to ensure that you are at least as good, if not better off, than if you were to use the "CPM" variant described above.

Cost per X This pricing method is primarily concerned with clicks, or click prices. There are different approaches and methods. With the cost per click (CPC) method, for example, you pay per click that is executed on the advertising medium. This is particularly common in the area of Google Ads. Furthermore, there is the Cost per Lead (CPL), which moves away from the individual clicks and deals more with the actual leads. The consumer site Comparis provides a good example here. If a customer makes a deal via the Comparis site, for example, this "lead" is paid for at a corresponding amount. The last variant is the so-called cost per order (CPO) option. CPO is the classic payment generated per completed purchase via advertising media.

Market participants and the distribution of roles

If we look at the market participants and their role distribution, it quickly becomes clear that each participant has its own role in the big picture. Let's start with the advertiser. He is actually the part that provides us with the budget. In return, there is the expectation that the desired and targeted advertising goal will be achieved without any problems. When we talk about agencies, they can be very different in terms of the form of specialization and possibilities. The goals of the agencies, however, are usually the same. The focus is on analysis, consulting, implementation and reporting. Agencies are often specialized, so there are agencies that only deal with email marketing, while others have their area more in social media, or even work with Google Ads.

In order to find the best agency for you, it is important to be clear in which direction you want to go. For example, an email agency will not necessarily understand performance marketing or vice versa. However, agencies also offer some advantages that you might not have if you do all the work in-house. For example, it is often the case that agencies use much more professional tools than is possible in-house. Agencies have a wealth of experience from other clients and the learnings that have come out of there. Operational blindness is also an issue that is often underestimated.

Agencies can shine there, too, because the big picture is easier for them to grasp. At the same time, we can also list optimization and reporting here. Another interesting point, depending on the size of the agency, are the corresponding purchasing conditions. (https://onma.de/werbeagentur-hannover/vorteile-und-nachteile-einer-werbeagentur/, n.d.)

Overview of performance marketing disciplines

Overview of Performance Marketing Disciplines Now let's take a look at the individual disciplines that performance marketing provides. I would like to show here the advantages and disadvantages of the individual possibilities in detail. -SEO (Search Engine Optimization) What is a big advantage of SEO is that there are no costs for agencies.

One saves thus some at budget and can use this then otherwise. The customer is already actively looking for e.g. a product (pull instead of push method) and will inevitably bring the conversion rate up. The trust that users already have in Google and its algorithms is very high, which can be seen as positive.

SEA (SEARCH ENGINE ADVERTISING)

Search engine advertising is charged via cost per click, which promises a good overview of the budget. Another advantage is that the advertising is flexible and can be cancelled at any time. It is possible to react to changes in the market or the product in a very timely manner. Here, too, pull instead of push takes place, which is ideal because the customer proactively searches for a product on his own.

Social media advertising
It's hard to imagine the advertising world without social media these days. However, there are a few things to keep in mind, especially in performance marketing, because each social media platform has its own requirements and may have a different audience.

If we look at Facebook at the start, we see that despite many doubters, it is still the platform with the highest general reach. A big advantage is the comment function, which allows active dialog with customers and thus promotes active exchange. In terms of branding and involvement, the platform is still one of the big players on the market and should not be underestimated. If we now go to Instagram, we see a somewhat different picture.

The reach is much higher than on Facebook, especially among the younger target group. High-quality images and videos can achieve a lot in this target group, especially in terms of branding. Twitter, on the other hand, is even more specific and especially popular in the media industry. The customer segment is completely different from Facebook or Instagram, for example.

Twitter is more of an information exchange platform than perhaps others. But especially in the customer service sector and in the B2B area, it's hard to imagine life without it. The last platform in the bunch is LinkedIn, which is very strong in HR and recruiting. For B2B professionals, this platform can also be interesting. There are still some special features, especially with regard to video ads on the social media platforms, which I would like to discuss.

You should keep in mind that most of the platforms today have an autoplay function. Many people watch the videos silently, for this reason subtitles should definitely find your place. It is important to remember that the actual brand should be shown as soon as possible, because the user often does not linger long on videos. Also, the length of a corresponding video should be around ten seconds, so the chance is much greater that the potential customer watches the video until the very end. (Newberry, 2019)

BANNERDESIGNS

Now that we've looked at social media platforms, I'd like to explain a few design-specific things about banner ads. Banners, those small windows that are mostly visible at the bottom of various pages, have some specific characteristics that I would like to point out here. Of course, it is very important that the banner fits the target group. It makes no sense to insert a car banner on a page for gardening supplies, because the target group is completely different.

A clear design and as simple a design as possible are in any case advantageous. Even small fonts can be disadvantageous if they are hardly legible. If images are inserted, it should be ensured that the advertising message itself is not pushed into the background. However, it is also the case that a good suitable image generates the attention of the potential customer.

The message itself should be well distinguished from the background in color, to avoid that the advertising itself is overlooked. It should also be considered that ani-mated banners are much more promising than static ones. However, there is also the possibility to animate only a part of the banner, which can also be advantageous.

EMAIL ADVERTISING FOR OUR STORE

Even today, email advertising is still the #1 most effective marketing discipline. Since we had actually never proactively promoted and implemented this in our company, we now wanted to make a start with email advertising to see if it would pay off. Also, the prospect of XY generating very good conversion rates gave us the impetus to start the trial.

Our first trial target group was to be existing customers. In other words, the customer stratum where upselling and cross-selling are an issue and where regular re-sales also take place. We sorted the existing customer base according to their product purchases. It is usually the case that a major customer orders printers for the entire company, for example. In our case it was also the case that an industrial company, which is one of our biggest customers, needed about 200 new printers.

Since we, as an outsourcing company, were responsible for the installation and maintenance of the selected devices, we were able to optimally prepare the newsletter in this course. We spoke fictitiously with the producer of the printers and were able to purchase the devices ourselves at an attractive preferential price. At the same time, the manufacturer assured us that he would be interested in sales for the printer cartridges of the respective type.

So we created a newsletter for the customer, where we first mentioned the attractive device prices. Underneath, we then advertised the printer cartridges as a subscription with the corresponding quantity. Based on the experience of the last few years, this was relatively easy to extract from the system data. We knew how many printer cartridges were normally used and were thus able to score twice. The customer was very pleased with the newsletter and immediately went for the cartridge subscription. It is often said that classic IT outsourcing is dead, but we cannot confirm this. If you can sell cartridges for 8500 printers at an attractive price, it is definitely worth it. For this reason, the newsletter definitely convinced us. (Campaignmonitor, 2020)

What we will try next in the area of email marketing is to engage the inactive customers more. This will then be rolled out company-wide in the form of a "Have you forgotten us?" mails including at-tractive offers at fair prices. The mail should also include a call-to-action button to encourage and inspire potential customers to buy again. Since we are planning this on a cross-national basis, we can also determine whether there are countries where this works less optimally than in others. This is certainly a kind of learning curve that we are paying, but it can be worthwhile in the long term.

NEUROMARKETING AND CONVERSION RATE OPTIMIZATION

What is neuromarketing about? It's about the psychological effect of a purchase decision. In other words, how do I get people to buy more because of my marketing measures, or to buy things that I didn't actually intend to buy? In the case of "herding", we as company XY actually didn't have to contribute much at all. We organized an event where all major partners were invited. The goal was to network and gather ideas. We took a closer look at our three largest companies to see what they had in common. We then highlighted these commonalities on stage, for example an innovation in the ordering system. And because of this constellation, smaller companies also wanted to discover this innovation for themselves. So Herding worked very well for us. For us in IT, certificates and quality seals are an indispensable part of the respective company. On the one hand, it radiates qualification and trust. And on the other hand, the customer is sure that only the best employees can be found there. For this reason, we are very prominent in the area of security, as well as in the SAP area.

We have also noticed that it is important to keep the awards and qualifications as up-to-date as possible. Once a certificate has expired, customers soon ask if we would renew it. So it already seems to be a need of the customer to work with a company that is up to date. We had never tried the "shortage" method before the course. So it was exciting to see if it would work. We started relatively small, generating a newsletter for a specific client.

Knowing "internally" that the customer was looking for new hard disks, we directed the newsletter to offer hard disks at a very good price. In a side sentence, it was prominently mentioned that we only had 100 left in stock and not to expect a new shipment for the time being.

I would say that an hour later the hard disks were all sold and the XY warehouse was empty. We didn't expect that, but it was a worthwhile test run for the company. The last topic in the area of neuromarketing, which we as a company have now pushed quite explicitly, is the so-called "steering through alternative price packages.

When we talk about service desk and customer service in our company, in the past it was always the case that the customer had purchased price X for this service from us, company XY. He was then bound and could not flexibly choose whether he needed an area, for example, the telephony or not. This was simply included in the package.

We now wanted to take a different approach by offering the customer appropriate packages with services that were more or less expensive for the customer depending on the effort involved. So that the customers were not overcharged, we defined four packages with a corresponding price and included services on our part. Internally, bets were made that it probably wouldn't work and that in the worst case we would have to add to the price if everyone switched to the cheapest package.

However, the phenomena that occurred were very positive, if unexpected. The majority of customers who had been paying relatively little until now switched to a more expensive package because they recognized the positive added value of the services listed and wanted to use them. The customers, who already use all our services, even on a large scale, suddenly wanted to know whether we could not put together a VIP package with a higher price, but where service XYZ would also be included.

This package is currently with us in the marketing department and in accounting to clarify how something like this could look. The amazing thing for me, however, is still that customers suddenly get a completely different understanding based on the listing of current services in terms of what would be possible.

Banner in company XY

As company XY, we've been asking ourselves for a long time how we should deal with the issue of banners. Does it really make sense for us as a company to take on the tedious work of proactively running banner ads? We wanted to dare the attempt and came after consultation with the marketing department to different approaches. That the banner should come in animated form was actually clear from the beginning. Static banners are not likely to attract many potential customers these days. It was also clear to us that the message had to be short, concise and to the point, so that someone would react positively to it. Also, a "Call to Action" button should not be missing, so that customers can take an action right away and generate a reaction. We learned in class that the customer stays on the banner for about two seconds until he turns away again. Therefore, we were well advised to convey the message as briefly as possible so that we could be sure that we had not already lost the customer somewhere. The banners will be up shortly, and for this reason I can't provide any field reports here yet. However, we are optimistic that this will also be a success and will further strengthen our position as a company. (Carmichael, 2020)

SEARCH ENGINE MANAGEMENT

The measurability of data in online marketing

I find this topic very exciting, because as an outsider I often had the feeling that every little piece of the puzzle in the big online marketing picture can be made measurable and visible. That this is not the case was shown to us, for example, by the presentation that tracking tools measure inaccurately by themselves. In addition, there is also the user behavior itself.

This is very individual and cannot be narrowed down. For example, users switch devices very frequently, from cell phones to laptops and then back to tablets. So you can roughly say that these measurements are trends that show the direction in which things are going. It is also becoming increasingly difficult in terms of cookies. Due to stricter data protection rules, analyses or even the targeting of users are almost impossible.

The importance of Google as a search engine

Up to six billion search queries are requested on the Google platform every day. Enormous computing power is required for this undertaking. Of course, a certain disadvantage arises if the Google website should fail for a short time, as it did in the summer of 2013. Within minutes, web traffic there plummeted by 40% simply because the site was unavailable.

And with over 85% market share, Google is, except for a few countries, certainly the market leader in search engines. In the year 2000, Google introduced AdWords, which finally enabled Google to generate money from the huge traffic. An interesting blog on this topic brought out the FAZ, which I would like to mention here. (Welter, 2013)

SEO (Search engine optimization)

So what is the goal of SEO in online marketing? It certainly tries first to ensure technical and content optimizations. Structural optimizations are also possible. Another main task is also to improve the ranking within relevant search terms. In general, one hopes for a broader audience.

That is, one would like to attract more visitors to the corresponding pages. And finally, the aim is to generate more leads or conversions, which in turn generate additional revenue. Especially in Switzerland, it is also in the specific area of SEO so that Google is certainly the main player. That is why most actions or inputs are automatically based on Google. The Google algorithm consists of over 200 different factors, which are in constant change and are also interchangeable.

TARGETING

When we talk about targeting, it is primarily about which keywords can be most accurately assigned to the appropriate target pages. For this reason, it makes no sense to push the keywords "car", for example, if the product itself is a motorcycle. It is also important to be aware that not only the target page itself should contain the product, but also all influenced sub-pages. These can be among others:

Category page
Subcategory page
Product detail page
Recipe page (e.g. if it is about a food product)
Advice page

Coming back to the "target page", we should note the following. Each target page has a single main thematic focus. This topic must be easy to find, on the one hand by the search engines themselves, and on the other hand for the user and potenial customer. We have now looked a bit at the topic of SEO and targeting, but what does it really take to make the ranking work? What really needs to be taken into account? And where are the biggest hurdles?

Important steps for the ranking boost on the Google search engine

Text types: The search engine recognizes the importance and relevance of the content on the basis of a text. The subject matter must therefore be clearly recognizably designed, so that the effect can unfold its maximum power.

Headings: When it comes to headlines, it is important to note that they are designed to be meaningful and short. It is also so that the headline occurs only once on the page and not used more often in the text.

Continuous texts: The continuous texts are the basics of the search engine to determine the appropriate relevance. It is therefore very important to capture it as correctly as possible. This starts with the correctness and also the thematic focus of the text. No less important are, among other things, the readability of the text and also uniqueness. Remember that you want to add value to the user, for example, in terms of timeliness or also to generate the reading benefit. (Bezboro-dova, May 21, 2019)

CRAWLING

Crawling is the process of finding and reading content on the web by triggering links to it. We have learned that good and useful linking facilitates crawling, because the search engine bots follow specific links. The crawling process can be controlled and influenced to the extent that the so-called ro-bots.txt file is included. In this specific file you can specify what exactly the crawler is looking for. This means that you tell the crawler which areas and sections of the corresponding website may be read and observed and which not. You can thus get a certain influence on the results.

INDEXING

When we talk about indexing, we are actually referring to the corresponding search results. This means that all relevant content may be used and evaluated for the corresponding search engines. However, it is also the case that non-relevant content may not be indexed, i.e. we exclude it. Relevant points are also, for example, whether the content and functions are ideally available for all devices (computer, cell phone, tablet). A website in a secure protocol (HTTPS) should also be available. In the international environment, it is important that the websites are declared country-specific. For Switzerland, for example, with the extension .ch or for Germany with the extension .de.

PAGE LOADING TIMES

We all know it. Slow websites or jerky videos that make us despair. Especially in the area of page load times, users have become spoiled. Thus, the page load times also play a major role in Google the longer, the more. Page load times can even be interpreted as a ranking factor. The performance of web pages and videos also influences usability. No customer will have much fun if the website takes forever to load, or even worse, crashes again and again due to programming errors or similar. For this reason it is important that the technical side is right. You save yourself a lot of trouble and make sure that Google's ranking factors are not negatively affected by abandonment rates, conversion rates that don't happen or even worse, problems with Google Ads.

SEA (SEARCH ENGINE ADVERTISING)

I would like to take the opportunity here again and generally come to speak on the subject of SEA. With the SEA, in German search engine advertising, the paid possibility of the advertisement of the text advertisements is described. Since these advertisements are switched via keyword, one can call this advertising form also Keyword Advertising. There are some big players among the providers of search engine advertising. Google Ads is of course at the forefront, followed by providers such as Bing Ads, Yandey Advertising and Baidu Advertising.

A decisive advantage of this type of advertising is certainly that the advertising campaign itself is created and prepared quite quickly. Also, the results are quick and easily measurable, which promises advertisers more accurate planning. When text ads are placed on Google Ads, for example, payment is made by click price. That is, the responsible advertiser effectively pays only if a visitor effectively clicks on the corresponding ad. Google Ads also offers different types of ad formats. It goes from text to the image ads, to the finished video ad. It should be noted, however, that especially with Google only a placement of text ads is possible. In order to really determine whether, for example, a conversion has taken place as a result of an Ads campaign, it is also recommended to use the "conversion tracking", which is integrated in the Ads account. (Smith, 2019)

Search Engine Marketing for company XY

What does the topic of search engine marketing mean for us as Company XY? How should we deal with it pro-actively and what benefits could we draw from what we have learned? First of all, we thought about how we could use our offers and products with search engine advertising. For this reason, we decided to proceed strategically and considered the following possibilities:

Markets: We checked those markets via Google Market Finder that seemed to be the most suitable for us. That is, the click prices should not be too high in relation. This should generate as much traffic as possible and use the full potential of the budget.

Audiences: Our main focus was on a specific customer group. On the one hand, we wanted to target customers who had already benefited from our services in the past, or who had at least visited our company homepage. We had to proceed in this way because we were quite tight on budget and always ran the risk of going over the maximum. In the end, the Google ads were shown to those users who were already active with us. At first, we feared that these customers would not notice the ads again and click because they had already purchased a service in the past. However, this concern remained unfounded.

Keywords: Here we were rather classical and only considered keywords that had a direct connection with us. Discussions arose within the company as to whether this would not be too restrictive and the like. In the end, however, we think that we made the right decision from the point of view of the big marketing goal. We included brand keywords as well as generic terms that generally covered the topics to be advertised. Since the IT industry in particular lives from many specific terms, these were also taken into account and implemented accordingly.

Display formats: Here we were very text-heavy. We wanted to avoid customers seeing too many image and video ads at all costs. Of course, this was also against the background of search engine optimization. -bids: A real war of beliefs broke out internally over the click bids. Many meant, one should enter nevertheless higher, so that one would get the appropriate offer at all to face. And still others, especially our management from accounting, for example, were of the opinion that you should go low, because otherwise the investment made in this campaign would not be recovered and the relationship to the profit would be impaired.

Conversions: The main goal of our company XY was to generate more conversions by optimizing the SEO/SEA activity. However, for a long time we did not know how to measure and report them correctly. For us as the marketing department, it was important to prove with facts and figures what this campaign in particular had brought to the company so far. Within Google Ads, there is a function called "conversion tracking". The function is presented with the help of a cookie, which is set on the user's computer, or rather the potential customer's computer. If the user clicks on the advertisement, for example, this is considered a conversion and is counted as a click on the advertisement. Of course, this is a relatively quick way to make results tangible. However, it should be noted that this is of course only the case if the cookie is installed. If it has already been removed by the user, the system will no longer have any reference and no active evaluation will be possible. -Search engine strategy: In order to decide on an advertising target and its benefits, we discussed in a large group who the targeted group should be. In addition to the geographical location, the language of the customers also played a role, as well as their interest in our services and products. (Doll, 2020)

DIGITAL ANALYTICS

What does the term digital analytics mean these days? The term "Google" is often used in this context because the tool "Google Analytics" has become a standard analytics program used by most parties. In general, however, the term "analytics" is about the following. It is about collecting, measuring and analyzing general digital data. It is meant to evaluate how the corresponding user behaves on websites, mobile sites, mobile apps, emails, social media platforms and also on the multiple search engines. It should also provide information about the "how and why".

For example, it can be questioned why certain AdWords are evaluated on a monthly basis, sometimes performing worse and sometimes better. Also the topic of reporting in this context should not remain unmentioned. Here a collection of indicators and warnings can be collected, which provides the user with various information. Generally speaking, it can be said that reporting is more concerned with the question of "what". For example, what has performed poorly or less well in the last month. All these different views and results of digital analytics uses the statistical modeling and concepts of data science.

One challenge in this area is certainly to ask the correct questions. What data can be collected? All of them, in principle. And which ones are useful and usable for us? Only a small subset, of the possible selection criteria. An interesting and useful distinction in this context is also "dimension vs. metric". When we talk about di-mension, in this context we mean the so-called descriptive characteristics of traffic. For example, "channel and demographics" are such dimensions. Inevitably, one cannot calculate with dimensions. The situation is different with metrics. These are behavioral characteristics of traffic, for example (visits to websites, abandonments, purchases via online stores), etc. These metrics can always be calculated. These metrics can always be calculated and used accordingly. (Cinalli, n.d.)

Help through tools

There are various tools that can be used to analyze and prepare data. The best known of these is undoubtedly "Google Analytics". This is a web and app analysis tool that provides data and information about the surfing behavior of customers. Another tool offered by Google is the "Google Data Studio", which is a tool that deals with reporting. The main task of "Google Data Studio" is to prepare data visually and make it understandable. You can use data from "Google Analytics", but it also works with other providers, such as Google Ads, Facebook, Instagram, etc.).

Google Analytics

I would like to talk about Google Analytics again here in particular. Google Analytics is the world's most widely used web analytics service for websites and is used by over 80 percent of all sites on the Internet. There are several other services that offer similar evaluations, but they never reached the range of Google Analytics. But what exactly does Google do differently or better? It is certainly the case that Google Analytics has gained its dominant market share by providing functions for free that were previously available for a fee or did not exist at all. Alternatives mentioned today are Adobe Analytics or Matomo.

If there is anything to criticize about Google Analytics from the user's point of view, it is at most the technical hurdle. It can quickly happen that inexperienced users, or users who come from a different environment, have problems with Google Analytics. For this reason, external help is often called in in the form of developers, for example.

What exactly is the added value of using Google Analytics? The data evaluation is huge and extensive and ranges from the simple evaluation of web pages to campaign tracking. For example, the age, gender, or even the length of time users spend on corresponding pages is often determined. Also the geographic location can be important to see which reach influence the given website has. The following additional important information can be retrieved via Google Analytics:

The amount of time visitors effectively spend on the website.

A number of web pages accessed in one session.

The bounce rate, i.e. the number of visitors who left the website without interacting with it.

Tracking of conversions: For example, that of sales or newsletter signups. But these can also be account adjustments or upgrades.

Measuring interactions: This looks at how often, for example, an embedded video is viewed by the visitor. You can quickly see whether this video, or audio files, have the desired effect or not.

It is also possible to collect important data and information via e-commerce tracking. This can be helpful under certain circumstances, with adjustments of products, or the Webshop itself. (Loup, 2020)

WHAT ARE KPI (KEY PERFORMANCE INDICATORS)

When we talk about KPIs, i.e. Key Performance Indicators, we are mainly talking about information such as measuring success in relation to specific activities. With KPIs it is mostly the case that it can be seen as an early warning system. It is therefore a kind of guide of success for activities carried out. Based on the evaluated KPIs, it is then possible to act and adjust accordingly.

LAW IN MARKETING AND COMMUNICATION

Points to note for a contract with influencers

If you want to work with influencers in the field of digital marketing, you should pay attention to a few important points. The subject of the agreement should specify which service is to be provided and within what framework. It should be drawn up in such a way that all parties involved find the contract comprehensible and acceptable. Further it is to be noted, from when to when the contract is active (running time of the contract). How should the remuneration take place and how will the service itself be carried out? What would happen in the event of illness or prevention of the order? Should a non-competition clause be included? If so, to what extent? What is decided in the contract on the subject of confidentiality? How is the return of documents and property regulated? Does a release from liability apply? There are also special final provisions to be included in the contract that would otherwise not fit any point. It should also be noted that influencer contracts may also contain specific contractual points that do not otherwise have to be listed.

For example, it must be regulated what happens in the event of a breach of contract. Image material that is protected by copyright must also be mentioned in the contract. What happens to postings and contributions in the social media area? These may have to be deleted again at a specified point, and this must also be visible in the contract.

For example, it must be regulated what happens in the event of a breach of contract. Image material that is protected by copyright must also be mentioned in the contract. What happens to postings and contributions in the social media area? Possibly these must be deleted again at a fixed point, this must also be visible in the contract. We have seen that the contract setup is very complex and adapted to the respective event. Therefore, it is definitely advantageous to consult a specialist who is familiar with the pitfalls and clauses of contract drafting. You save both parties a lot of time and don't run the risk of putting your foot in your mouth, which you were not aware of before.

The EU GDPR and Swiss companies

Since the amendment of the GDPR, there have been some changes that affect not only the European Union, but also Switzerland. The following points are crucial for the data processing of a Swiss company to fall under the GDPR and be directly affected by it. - The Swiss company must have an establishment in one of the EU countries. - The Swiss company offers services or goods in the EU area. For example, this can be done via a webshop. - The Swiss company monitors the behavior of its customers in the European area (e.g. the surfing behavior on the web pages, etc.) In this way, personalized offers can also be made.

Art. 6 of the DSGVO Legality and data processing

This article quite tricky and detailed. For this reason, I will go over the most important points again here. The data subject must have given his or her mandatory consent for the processing of personal data. Data subjects also have key rights under the GDPR that must be complied with.

The "right to erasure" also applies here. This means nothing other than that data must be deleted if it has fulfilled its purpose and is no longer needed. This is also called the right to be forgotten. This is intended to prevent data from being passed on to other people, even if they have no connection with it. (Honecker, 2020)

Law in marketing and communication for company XY

Although we as company XY have quite a large legal department, we have to admit that it is rather general. It tries to meet the needs of all branches on an international level, but it does it more badly than it should. The main problem is that each country has different demands on the legal department and they are supposed to cover an area from Singapore to Frankfurt and Basel. Quasi a thing of the impossibility. For this reason, among others, the legal department gives us a relatively large amount of freedom, or, in other words, hopes that we will take responsibility for ourselves.

So, internally, we first went through all the contracts, whether from a marketing point of view or also with external ones that have a communicative connection with us. We quickly saw that we had a number of gaps that were not covered, at least contractually. No damage had yet been done, but we wanted to keep it that way. That's why we systematically went through all the contracts. Since we also work with influencer marketing, among other things, this was our first point of reference for the audit. The first thing we noticed was that, for example, we had not declared a clear start and end date for the duration of the contract. This was changed so that this gap could also be closed. For contracts that are now newly concluded, some points have generally been added. For example, it is now included that the return of documents and property must take place no later than the last day of the contractually defined date.

In this way, we also ensure internally that confidential data and documents on new projects or offers do not circulate outside our branch. The non-competition clause has also been tightened up and adapted. In the past, we were somewhat naive and imprudent in this area. But we have learned from this and the holes that appeared have been closed. For example, it is now stipulated that there must be no direct competition of products from us to another supplier for at least one year. (Gosemann, 2018) Another delicate issue that we simply did not pay attention to in the past was to consider the corresponding image and video materials as our company property. Especially today where people quickly post, delete and comment on all social media platforms, this is extremely important. In the past, it was rather the case that we verbally instructed the contractual partner to be careful with the images and videos as far as their distribution was concerned. But could we be sure that this was how it was lived? And even if we were to learn of misuse of the films and photos by chance or something similar, what should we do? We had virtually addressed this issue in a conversation with the influencer and then put it back in a box. The new situation is that all issues relating to image rights, sound rights and video rights are clearly regulated in the contract. We have already noticed a change in the behavior of the respective contractual partner in this regard, which I would not have thought. Whereas in the past this topic was discussed rather casually, today it is noticeably the case that the contracting partner is much more and much more deeply involved in the matter and wants to know what the individual clauses and notes within the contract mean. The consequences are also generally discussed more and more intensively. In the end, it is now much clearer for all parties and we as a company do not run the risk of running into problems afterwards. We have also made contractual adjustments regarding the deletion and removal of posts. The conditions have become much stricter and more direct, because we want our contractual partners to understand that posts can have a major impact on the positive outcome of a campaign and we definitely want to exclude any problems with this.

Google Analytics in the XY company environment

To put it bluntly, company XY is not exactly a god when it comes to using Google Analytics. On the one hand, the main focus is more on customer service and product sales in the old style, i.e. with acquisition via telephone, or direct customer contact on site. On the other hand, we are only at the beginning of digital marketing strategies. Since this digital marketing training course has given us such a boost, it's only natural that we would also like to take a closer look at Google Analytics to understand whether our feeling is correct or not.

It is often the case that you have a good feeling about an action, but can you prove it with numbers? Rather rarely, and so that's where Google Analytics comes in. The first thing we did was to start generating periodic reports that are automatically emailed to us. This allows us to review the relevant metrics and adjust and change them as needed.

It was very important to us to get a big picture of what we could finally evaluate. So we started to measure the number of page views and from which website the visitors came to our own website. Then we looked at how much time the visitors were willing to spend on our site. In this context, we also examined how high the bounce rate was.

This is the number of visitors who left our website without interacting with it. All this information provided by Google Analytics made us smarter about our own website handling. For example, we never had in mind to filter users by their geolocation. But this made sense, because we noticed that many French-speaking people visit the site and we were doing a poor job with the translation. What I also find quite interesting is that Google Analytics can be integrated with Google Ads. This generates some advantages, be it on the statistical level, or also in terms of optimization through corresponding Google Ads campaigns. (Demers, 2020)

Epilogue

I hope that the content of this book has provided the information you were looking for. Digital marketing is all about trial and error, gaining experience, testing and retesting. Make your own strategies and plans and don't be afraid to question all processes, even critically. I have tried to include as much content as possible without becoming too theoretical. Nevertheless, I hope that this book will give you as much content as a course, which often costs a lot of money.

I would be very happy to receive a review from you on Amazon. This is the only way I know where I stand and can improve and keep this book current. I wish you much success in implementing your digital marketing plans.

Your Gilles Kroeger

Bibliography

The Boston Consulting Group, Business Model Innovation (2009), abgerufen von https://image-src.bcg.com/Images/BCG_Business_Model_Innovation_Dec_09_tcm56-121706.pdf

Dr. Hoffmann/J. / Rook/S., 18.03.2018, Das 3-Horizonte Modell für mehr Innovation, abgerufen von https://upload-magazin.de/23657-3-horizonte-modell/

Chesbrough/H.,2010, Business Model Innovation Opportunities and Barriers, abgerufen von http://www.businessmodelcommunity.com/fs/Root/8oex8-Chesbrough.pdf

Wehr/A., 13.12.18, Wie Business Model Innovation zu nachhaltigen Kundenbeziehung führt, abgerufen von https://www.tractionwise.com/magazine/business-model-innovationkundenfokus/

Tyreholt/P, 20.12.2017, Digital transformation requires business model innovation, abgerufen von https://www.cybercom.com/About-Cybercom/Blogs/Business-and-technology-intheconnected-world/digital-transformation-requires-business-model-innovation-1-of-3/

Dr. Eckert/R., 12.11.16, Business Model Prototype – Der Kern des Geschäftsmodells, abgerufen von http://www.hyperwettbewerb.com/new-blog/2016/12/11/business-model-prototype-oderdie-hypothese-vom-geschftsmodellkern-1

Benjamin, (26. Juni 2019) LinkedIN für Gründer: Brauche ich das Netzwerk für meinen Erfolg? Abgerufen von https://www.fuer-gruender.de/blog/linkedin-fuer-gruender-basics/

Bloom, D. (15. Mai 2020). Die Vor- und Nachteile von Twitter. Abgerufen von https://www.blumerang.com/die-vor-und-nachteile-von-twitter

Chen. (3. Oktober 2017). Tips on branding your YouTube channel. Abgerufen von https://artplusmarketing.com/tips-on-branding-your-youtube-channel-3f67f4f2ca00

Firsching, J. (17. November 2017). Instagram Stories jetzt auch auf dem Desktop. Abgerufen von https://www.futurebiz.de/artikel/instagram-stories-desktop/

Firsching, J. (14. November 2018). Instagram Stories. Wie Unternehmen Instagram Stories einsetzen sollten. Abgerufen von https://www.futurebiz.de/artikel/instagram-stories-tippsunternehmen/

Franklin, J. (4. September 2019). How to effectively use LinkedIn for Brand awareness. Abgerufen von https://themanifest.com/social-media/how-effectively-use-linkedin-brand-awareness

Lawal, M. (1. August 2018). 23 Vorteile, die Social Media für Unternehmen bietet. Abgerufen von https://blog.hootsuite.com/de/vorteile-von-social-media-fuer-unternehmen/

Mitter, S. (2020). Website vs. Facebook – Die Vorteile & Nachteile für KMU. Abgerufen von https://www.prospega.de/de/mediaratgeber/fachartikel/facebook-vs-webseiten-kmu

Smith, K. (3. März 2020) 57 interessante Zahlen und Statistiken rund um YouTube. Abgerufen von https://www.brandwatch.com/de/blog/statistiken-youtube/

Stark, N. (4. Dezember 2018). 6 Vorteile von Pinterest für dein Unternehmen. Abgerufen von https://www.pergenz.de/blog/6-vorteile-von-pinterest-fuer-unternehmen/

Statista. (2020).Abgerufen von https://de.statista.com/statistik/daten/studie/70221/umfrage/anzahl-der-nutzer-von-facebook-inder-schweiz/

Weiss, J (2017), Die wichtigsten Socialmedia Plattformen- ein Überblick, Abgerufen von https://blog.mediakraft.de/some-uebersicht-86bec97a7d0c

digitalmarketinginstitute.com/. (o.D). How to write a Video Marketing script. Abgerufen von https://digitalmarketinginstitute.com/en-eu/blog/how-to-write-a-video-marketing-script

Hilker, U. (2020). Digital Marketing Strategie mit Crossmedia Kampagnen Beispiele. Abgerufen von https://www.hilker-consulting.de/digital-marketing/digital-marketing-strategie-mitcrossmedia-kampagnen-beispiele

Lotse, M. (13. August 2019). Die eigene Video Ausrüstung - So gelingt der Dreh im Unternehmen! Abgerufen von https://blog.mark-lotse.com/das-eigene-home-video-studio-auf-dieseausr%C3%BCstung-kommt-es-an

marketingimpott.de. (2020). Die Herausforderungen einer Crossmedia-Kampagne. Abgerufen von https://www.marketingimpott.de/blog/die-herausforderungen-einer-crossmedia-kampagne/

Teamblau. (20. Mai 2020). Storytelling im YouTube Zeitalter: Die Macht der visuellen Geschichten. Abgerufen von https://www.teamblau.com/de/storytelling-youtube--1-2180.html

Theobald, T. (12. November 2018). Foto- vs. Video-Content Von diesen Faktoren hängt der Erfolg von Instagram Kampagnen ab. Abgerufen von https://www.horizont.net/marketing/nachrichten/foto--vs.-video-content-von-diesen-faktorenhaengt-der-erfolg-von-instagram-kampagnen-ab-171021

https://www.cyberclick.net/marketing/performance-marketing/. (o.D). Discover what Performance Marketing is! Abgerufen von https://www.cyberclick.net/marketing/performancemarketing

https://onma.de/werbeagentur-hannover/vorteile-und-nachteile-einer-werbeagentur/. (o.D). Vorteile und Nachteile einer Werbeagentur. Abgerufen von https://onma.de/werbeagenturhannover/vorteile-und-nachteile-einer-werbeagentur/

Newberry, C. (06. Juni 2019). Social Media Advertising 101: How to get the most out of Your Ad budget. Abgerufen von https://blog.hootsuite.com/social-media-advertising/

Campaignmonitor.com. (2020). How Email can improve your inbound marketing strategy. Abgerufen von https://www.campaignmonitor.com/blog/email-marketing/2020/07/how-email-canimprove-your-inbound-marketing-strategy/

https://www.newneuromarketing.com. (09. Juni 2020). Why we're blind to our best ideas. Abgerufen von https://www.newneuromarketing.com/

Carmichael, K. (29. Oktober 2019) How to explain Banner Ads to anyone. Abgerufen von https://blog.hubspot.com/marketing/banner-ad-clicks

Welter, P. (01. April 2013) Monopol aus eigener Leistung. Abgerufen von https://blogs.faz.net/fazit/2013/04/01/monopol-aus-eigener-leistung-1349

Bezborodova, E. (21. Mai 2019) Blog-SEO: 17 Tipps zur Verbesserung des Google Rankings. Abgerufen von https://www.lianatech.de/ressourcen/blog/blog-seo-17-tipps-zur-verbesserungdes-google-rankings.html

Smith, B. (08. Oktober 2019) Google Ads 101 – The guide that takes you from zero to hero. Abgerufen von https://adespresso.com/blog/google-ads/

Doll, M. (07. Januar 2020) Was ist Suchmaschinenwerbung? SEA einfach erklärt. Abgerufen von https://www.luna-park.de/blog/36368-was-ist-suchmaschinenwerbung-sea-einfach-erklaert/

Leist, R. (27. Juli 2020) How to do Keyword reseach for SEO: A beginner's guide. Abgerufen von https://blog.hubspot.com/marketing/how-to-do-keyword-research-ht

Gerloff, J. (09. September 2020) SEO: Warum fortlaufende Optimierung so wichtig ist. Abgerufen von https://www.contentmanager.de/seo-sem/seo-warum-fortlaufende-optimierung-sowichtig-ist/

Cinalli, B. (o.D) Understanding Google Analytics: What are Dimensions, Metrics & Bounce rate?. Abgerufen von https://www.forwardpmx.com/insights/blog/what-are-google-analyticsdimensions-metrics/

Loup, A. (07. April 2020) Google Analytics – Einblicke in Googles beliebtes Webanalyse-Tool. Abgerufen von https://www.luna-park.de/blog/36826-googleanalytics/#:~:text=Das%20in%20der%20Basis%2DVersion,Standort%20von%20Website%2DBesuch ern%2C%20sowie

Honecker, M. (25. Juli 2020) DSGVO für Blogger und Webseitenbetreiber – das musst du wissen. Abgerufen von https://martinahonecker.com/dsgvo-leitfaden/

Gosemann, L. (18. Juli 2018) Online Marketing nach der DSGVO: Das ist zu beachten. Abgerufen von https://www.publishingblog.ch/gastbeitrag-online-marketing-nach-der-dsgvo-das-ist-zubeachten/

Demers, T. (11. Juni 2020) Quick guide to Google Analytics reporting in Google Adwords. Abgerufen von https://www.wordstream.com/blog/ws/2012/04/05/google-analytics-reporting-inadwords

Egli, T. (28. Juli 2020) Ecommerce tracking with Google Analytics. Abgerufen von https://blog.xeit.ch/2020/07/google-analytics-ecommerce/

www.ingramcontent.com/pod-product-compliance
Lightning Source LLC
Chambersburg PA
CBHW072144170526
45158CB00004BA/1508